GW01185454

This Book Belongs To

_____

As you open this book and begin your journey into self-discovery, think about what your goals are. What is it that you hope to gain from your journaling experience? Are you trying to gain a better understanding of yourself? Do you wish to develop new coping mechanisms? Whatever your goals are, know that you are taking a step in the right direction. The hope is that you will use this book as a tool for spiritual clarity and growth in all areas of your life.

1

Name three people you are grateful to have in your life. Why did you choose these people?

Date : _____

Name three things you are grateful to have in your life. Why did you choose these things?

3

Name three things you love
about yourself. Why did you
choose these things?

Date : _____

4

Name something you'd like to
change about yourself. Why do
you want to change this thing?

Date : _____

Name something you'd like to change about your life. Why do you want to change this thing?

Date : _____

What have you done to change the things you wished were different about yourself?

Date : _____

What have you done to change
the things you wished were
different about your life ?

Date : _____

8

What do you enjoy doing during your free time?

Date : _____

What is something you wish you had more time to do?

10

Do you consider yourself to be someone who uses your time wisely?

Date : _____

What are some ways that you could make better use of your time?

_____

_____

_____

_____

_____

_____

_____

_____

_____

_____

_____

_____

_____

_____

_____

_____

_____

Who do you enjoy spending time with?

Date : _____

13

Name someone in your life you'd
like to spend more time with.
How can you make that happen?

Date : _____

Name someone who makes you smile when you think of them (past or present relationship).

Date : _____

Name someone who makes you
angry when you think of them
(past or present relationship).

Date : _____

16

Name someone who makes you sad when you think of them (past or present relationship).

Date : _____

Name someone or something that makes you laugh.

Date : _____

What is the happiest memory
you have of your childhood?

Date : _____

What is the saddest memory you have of your childhood?

Date : _____

What is the funniest memory you have of your childhood?

Date : _____

What is the happiest memory you have from your adult life?

What is the saddest memory you have from your adult life?

Date : _____

What is the funniest memory you have from your adult life?

_____

_____

_____

_____

_____

_____

_____

_____

_____

_____

_____

_____

_____

_____

_____

_____

_____

_____

Date : _____

Describe yourself as a child.
What was your personality like?
What things did you enjoy?

Date : _____

Describe yourself as a teenager.
What was your personality like?
What things did you enjoy?

Describe yourself as an adult.

Do you recognize any similarities when you compare yourself as a child, teenager and an adult?

Date : _____

Do you recognize any differences when you compare yourself as a child, teenager and an adult?

Date : _____

Are you the person you thought you'd grow up to be?

Date : _____

How is your life different from
how you imagined it would be
when you were a child?

_____

_____

_____

_____

_____

_____

_____

_____

_____

_____

_____

_____

_____

_____

_____

What is something you worked
really hard to achieve/earn?

How did you feel when you finally got that thing you worked so hard for?

How did your life change when you finally got that thing you worked so hard for?

Date : _____

What is something you think you failed at?

Thinking about the thing you failed at (#34), is it something you'd give another try?

What was the best job you've had? What did you like about it?

Date : _____

What was your least favorite
job? What did you not like
about it?

Do you enjoy your current job?
Why or why not?

Date : _____

Describe your dream job?

_____
_____
_____
_____
_____
_____
_____
_____
_____
_____
_____
_____
_____
_____
_____
_____
_____
_____

40

Who/what is stopping you from having the dream job you wrote about for #39?

How is your dream job different
from the job you currently have?
How are they the same?

42

What changes could you make in your life to make your dream job a reality?

Date : _____

If you could travel to anyplace
in the world, where would it
be and why?

Thinking about #43, who would
you bring with you and why?

Thinking about #43, who would definitely not be invited and why?

Think about someone who had a positive impact on your life. What would you like to say to them?

What is the most important issue in your life right now?

Date : _____

Who is the most important person in your life right now?

_____
_____
_____
_____
_____
_____
_____
_____
_____
_____
_____
_____
_____
_____
_____
_____

What is your greatest fear?

Date : _____

50

Name one thing you can do to overcome the fear you mentioned in #49.

Date : _____

What was the best moment of your day today?

What do you feel is missing in your life?

If you were just given $1 million, what's the first thing you would do with the money?

Date : _____

What do you enjoy spending your money on?

Date : _____

What do you spend most of
your money on?

Date : _____

Do you consider yourself to be good with money?

What was the last major purchase you made? How did it change your life?

Date : _____

Describe something nice you did for someone else.

Date : _____

Describe something nice
someone else did for you.

Describe the last time you cried.

Date : _____

Describe the last time you laughed.

Describe the last time you got
into an argument.

Describe your last birthday.

How did you spend your last major holiday? Who did you spend it with?

Describe an unhealthy habit
that you wish you could quit.

Name two things you could do to help you quit your unhealthy habit (#65).

Date : _____

Name a healthy habit that you've made a part of your daily life.

Think about the habit you mentioned in #67. Why is it important to you?

Date : _____

What is something you need to
work harder at...something you
know you could be better at?

70

Is there anyone in your life that you envy? What is it about this person that makes you envious?

What's the most adventurous thing you've ever done?

What is your greatest strength?

What is your greatest weakness?

Write about someone you
admired as a child.

Date : _____

Write about someone you admired as an adult or currently admire.

Date : _____

Who was your childhood best friend? Are you still friends today?

Date : _____

How was your relationship with your parents growing up?

How is your relationship with your parents right now?

Date : _____

How was your relationship with your siblings/other family members growing up?

80

How is your relationship with your siblings/other family members right now?

Write about a time in your life
when you felt afraid.

Write about a time in your life
when you felt anxious/worried.

Write about a time in your life
when you felt depressed.

Write about a time in your life
when you felt lonely.

Write about a time in your life
when you felt unsure about
someone/something.

Date : _____

Write about a time in your life when you felt contentment.

Date : _____

Write about a time in your life
when you felt most at peace.

Write about a time in your life when you experienced joy.

Write about a time in your life
when you felt loved.

Date : _____

Write about someone or something you really miss.

_____

_____

_____

_____

_____

_____

_____

_____

_____

_____

_____

_____

_____

_____

_____

_____

Name something that made
you smile in the past week.

Date : _____

Name something that frustrated you in the past week.

Name a goal you set for
yourself in the past week that
you accomplished.

Date : _____

Name a goal you set for yourself in the past week that you didn't accomplish.

Think about #94. Why didn't you accomplish that goal? Can you accomplish it this week?

Date : _____

Name a personality trait you wish you had.

Name a personality trait that
you have, but wish you didn't.

Date : _____

Write about something you're looking forward to.

Date : _____

What piece of advice would you give your teenage self?

Date : _____

If you had to choose a different career, what career would you choose?

Date : _____

If you could change one thing about your day today, what would it be and why?

If you could know one thing about your future, what would it be?

Date : _____

If you could go back in time and change one decision you made, what would it be?

Date : _____

If you could speak to one person who is no longer in your life, who would it be? What would you say?

Date : _____

If you had a magic genie, what
would your three wishes be?

Name three things you want to
do before you die.

Name one thing you haven't done because of fear.

If you wrote a thank you note to yourself, what would it say?

If you wrote a thank you note to
your parents, what would it say?

Date : _____

Where do you see yourself in one year from now?

Date : _____

Where do you see yourself in
five years from now?

Where do you see yourself in ten years from now?

Date : _____

Where do you see yourself in
twenty years from now?

What could you do today
instead of looking at your phone?

What was your greatest challenge over the past year?

What was your greatest achievement over the past year?

What/who keeps you motivated?

Date : _____

What did you do for yourself today?

Date : _____

What did you do for others
today?

Date : _____

How can you make tomorrow better than today?

Date : _____

What is your favorite way to start the day and why?

Date : _____

What is your favorite way to end
the day and why?

_____

_____

_____

_____

_____

_____

_____

_____

_____

_____

_____

_____

_____

_____

Date : _____

What would your ideal day look like?

Date : _____

Write down a positive phrase
that you can repeat to yourself
during stressful situations.

Date : _____

What is your most unrealistic worry?

What are some ways that you stay connected to those who are important to you?

Date : _____

What is the best compliment
you've ever received? Who gave
you the compliment?

What is the best gift you've ever received? Who gave you the gift?

What is your biggest character flaw?

What is your favorite thing about yourself?

Date : _____

What is the biggest life lesson
you've learned so far?

Date : _____

What was the most stressful part of your day today?

Date : _____

What was the most peaceful
part of your day today?

134

Describe yourself in two words. Why did you choose those words?

Describe your life in two words.
Why did you choose those
words?

What are some changes you could make to be healthier?

Date : _____

What's stopping you from making the healthy changes you mentioned in #136?

When you go to bed at night, what do you find yourself thinking about?

Have you ever had a recurring dream? What was it about?

List three people you enjoy talking to. Why did you choose those people?

Name two ways you could step
outside of your comfort zone
this week.

Write about a time when you
had to apologize to someone.

_____

_____

_____

_____

_____

_____

_____

_____

_____

_____

_____

_____

_____

_____

_____

_____

Write about a time when you
had to forgive someone.

Write about a time when you
had to confront someone.

When are you your happiest?

When are you your least patient self?

Date : _____

When are you most productive?

What is something you're very proud of?

If you could go back to being a child (age 5-12) for just one day, how would you spend that day?

If you could go back to being a teenager for just one day, how would you spend that day?

151

When you think about your childhood days, what feelings do you experience?

Date : _____

Have you ever wrongly judged someone before getting to know them? Who was the person?

Date : _____

When was the last time you did something really fun? Write about that experience.

What does gratitude mean to you? Is it something that comes easy for you?

Date : _____

Name something that made you laugh this week.

Write about something you're really good at.

Who do you lean on during difficult times? Why do you lean on this person?

Date : _____

What family traditions (past or present) do you really enjoy?

Date : _____

What does home mean to you?

Date : _____

What do you most enjoy about your home?

161

What would you like to change about your home? Why?

Write about something that you have now, but you didn't have as a child.

Date : _____

Write about an obstacle in your
life that you overcame.

Describe a bad experience that made you stronger.

_____
_____
_____
_____
_____
_____
_____
_____
_____
_____
_____
_____
_____
_____
_____
_____
_____

Date : _____

What cheers you up when
you're feeling low?

Date : _____

166

If you could be the best in the world at one thing, what would it be and why?

What's the best advice you've ever received?

Write about a book, movie, or song that had a big impact on your life.

Date : _____

Write about a person that
had a big impact on your life.

What do you want people to
say about you after you're
gone?

Date : _____

What's the most embarassing
thing that ever happened
to you?

_____

_____

_____

_____

_____

_____

_____

_____

_____

_____

_____

_____

_____

_____

_____

_____

Pick a positive word to focus on
this week (strength, love, etc.)
Why did you choose this word?

Date : _____

Write about an experience when
you felt that someone wronged
you.

Write about how you're feeling
right now, at this very moment.

Date : _____

What qualities are important to you in a friendship?

What qualities are important to you in a romantic relationship?

What qualities are important for you, yourself, to have?

Date : _____

If you could live anyplace in the world, where would it be and why?

Who/what is stopping you from living in the place you mentioned in the previous question?

Date : _____

What is something nobody knows about you? Why have you not shared this with anyone?

181

Finish this sentence: My life would be incomplete without...

What difficult thoughts or emotions come up for you most often?

Date : _____

How do you handle difficult emotions?

184

What parts of your daily life cause the most stress or frustration?

Date : _____

Thinking about #184, what can you do to make these areas of your life less stressful?

_____

_____

_____

_____

_____

_____

_____

_____

_____

_____

_____

_____

_____

_____

_____

_____

_____

What does your self-talk sound like? Do you engage in self-defeating thoughts?

How can you reframe negative self-talk to keep yourself encouraged?

Do you prioritize self-care?
Name some of your self-care
activities?

Date : _____

189

Name something about adulthood
that surprised you...something you
didn't expect to experience/feel.

Date : _____

What are your goals for this week? Do you think you can realistically achieve these goals?

What are the obstacles that might keep you from achieving the goals from #190?

Name something that made you laugh or smile this week.

Date : _____

What person or thing were you most grateful for this week?

Date : _____

What did you do to relax or unwind this week?

_____

_____

_____

_____

_____

_____

_____

_____

_____

_____

_____

_____

_____

_____

_____

_____

_____

Date : _____

Name three things you can do differently to improve the next week of your life.

Name someone who drains your
energy. How can you improve
your interactions with him or her?

Date : _____

What is something you wish you didn't have to do today? How will you feel once it's over?

_____

_____

_____

_____

_____

_____

_____

_____

_____

_____

_____

_____

_____

_____

_____

Do you have any hobbies? If not, what is a hobby you might be interested in?

Date : _____

Name three things you accomplished this week that you feel good about.

Date : _____

Finish this sentence: Today I am looking forward to...

Date : _____

What are the most used apps on
your phone? How do they add
value to your life?

Date : _____

What are some things you take for granted?

Date : _____

What is something you feel passionate about...something you enjoy doing or talking about?

Date : _____

Which of your relationships do you put the most energy into (marriage, parenthood, etc.)?

Date : _____

When you think about your
future, are you more excited or
more scared and why?

_____
_____
_____
_____
_____
_____
_____
_____
_____
_____
_____
_____
_____
_____
_____
_____
_____
_____
_____
_____

Date : _____

Name something you need to forgive yourself for.

Date : _____

What are some ways you can serve your community?

_____
_____
_____
_____
_____
_____
_____
_____
_____
_____
_____
_____
_____
_____
_____
_____
_____

Are there areas of your life in which you are too hard on yourself?

Date : _____

Have there been times when
you've been too hard on others?

Talk about a time when you felt you didn't belong or didn't fit in.

Date : _____

Talk about a time when you struggled with something or someone?

_____

_____

_____

_____

_____

_____

_____

_____

_____

_____

_____

_____

_____

_____

_____

_____

Date : _____

Name something you could do
to simplify your life.

Date : _____

Do you consider yourself more
of a minimalist or a maximalist?

Are you more of a spender or a
saver? Why?

If you could only accomplish
three things today, what would
they be?

Date : _____

Name something that makes you uncomfortable.

Date : _____

What is a big project that you've
been too intimidated to start?

Name one step you can take to get started with your big project (#217).

219

Name something you could
achieve if you had more help.
Who might be able to help you?

Date : _____

What are you willing to sacrifice
now to have your dream life
later?

What negative things have people said about you? Do you believe these things?

What positive things have people said about you? Do you believe these things?

Date : _____

223

If you keep doing the same things you're doing, will you be closer to your dream life next year?

Date : _____

Finish this letter: Dear Past Me,

_____
_____
_____
_____
_____
_____
_____
_____
_____
_____
_____

_____
_____
_____
_____

Date : _____

Finish this letter: Dear Future Me,

Date : _____

Finish this sentence: The most
surprising moment of my life...

Finish this sentence: The most disappointing moment of my life...

Date : _____

Finish this sentence: The saddest moment of my life...

Date : _____

What is your favorite weekend
activity?

_____

_____

_____

_____

_____

_____

_____

_____

_____

_____

_____

_____

_____

_____

_____

_____

_____

230

How easy is it for you to forgive those who've caused you pain? Do you hold grudges?

Date : _____

What is your earliest memory?

As a child, who was your favorite relative and why?

Date : _____

Who or what made you feel
good this week?

Date : _____

What did you do this week that moved you closer to your goals?

Date : _____

When did you feel truly
independent for the first time?

Date : _____

What would you do if you could
live a day without consequences?

_____
_____
_____
_____
_____
_____
_____
_____
_____
_____
_____
_____
_____
_____
_____
_____

If you could snap your fingers and change one thing, what would it be?

238

What great adventure do you wish you could go on?

If you could change three things about the world, what would they be?

Date : _____

How would your best friend describe you?

How would your family describe you?

Date : _____

What first impression do you
think others have of you?

Describe your parents upbringing?

Date : _____

Thinking about #243, what affect did your parents upbringing have on the way they raised you?

Date : _____

Finish this sentence: I got where I
am today because...

Do you have any strengths or talents that are not being used at the moment?

Date : _____

Are you a perfectionist? Do you believe in perfection?

Date : _____

248

Finish this sentence: I need to accept that...

Finish this sentence: I need to spend more time...

Date : _____

Finish this sentence: I need to spend less time...

Date : _____

What is the hardest thing you've ever had to do? Why was it hard for you?

What are three fears you've
overcome as you've matured?

Date : _____

What are three weaknesses
you've overcome as you've
matured?

_____

_____

_____

_____

_____

_____

_____

_____

_____

_____

_____

_____

_____

_____

_____

_____

_____

_____

Have you ever been in love? How did you know you were in love? Write about that experience.

What does it mean to have a
soul mate? Are soul mates real?

Do you need to be in a relationship to be happy/content with your life?

What was the last kind thing
you did for someone else?

What was the last kind thing you did for yourself?

Date : _____

What do you dislike most about being an adult?

Date : _____

What do you like most about being an adult?

Date : _____

What do you miss the most about being a child?

_____
_____
_____
_____
_____
_____
_____
_____
_____
_____
_____
_____
_____
_____
_____
_____
_____
_____

If you had to leave everything behind, and could only take 3 **things**, what would you take?

Date : _____

How are you feeling today?
What made you feel that way?

Name something positive in your
life that you have, but many
people don't have.

What is the last new thing you tried? How was that experience?

Date : _____

How do you deal with failure or rejection?

If you could invent one thing
that would change people's lives,
what would it be?

Date : _____

If your body could speak, what would it tell you?

Date : _____

Finish this sentence: I am so blessed to be able to...

Finish this sentence: I am going to try to be better at...

Date : _____

What are your goals for today?

Date : _____

What are your goals for this week?

What is your favorite quote?
Why do you like this quote?

Date : _____

If you had an extra hour in your day, how would you use your time?

Date : _____

If you came with a warning label,
what would it say?

Name three things your dream home would have to have. Why are those things important?

Describe the past experience
you learned the most from.

Date : _____

Finish this sentence: I feel I'm at
my best when...

_____

_____

_____

_____

_____

_____

_____

_____

_____

_____

_____

_____

_____

_____

_____

Date : _____

If you could live inside one TV show, what would it be?

_____
_____
_____
_____
_____
_____
_____
_____
_____
_____
_____
_____
_____
_____
_____
_____
_____
_____

280

Describe the strongest emotion you felt today. Give details.

List three childhood memories
you're grateful to have.

Date : _____

Name one difficult thing that happened to you, but you're now grateful for that experience.

Date : _____

Did you make healthy choices today? Talk about the healthy or unhealthy decisions you made.

Date : _____

What is your relationship with exercise? How often do you exercise? What do you enjoy?

What are your fitness and health goals?

Do you have a family history of any chronic illnesses? How has that impacted your life?

What kind of person do you
aspire to be?

Date : _____

Do your current friendships and
relationships bring you joy?

_____

_____

_____

_____

_____

_____

_____

_____

_____

_____

_____

_____

_____

_____

_____

_____

_____

_____

289

In what ways could you be a better friend, partner, sibling, son/daughter, etc.?

Date : _____

Do you think you are a positive or a negative person?

Describe something that can
quickly turn your mood from
positive to negative.

When you're in a bad mood, how long do you stay there? How do you come out of it?

Date : _____

What is the most important thing you need to achieve this week?

Name something you can do to make tomorrow better than today.

Date : _____

If you could have any
superpower, what would it be?
How would you use your power?

Date : _____

Describe an item you own that means a lot to you. Why is this item important to you?

297

If you had to spend an entire day
doing only one thing, what would
it be and why?

What is your relationship with religion?

Date : _____

Do you believe in a higher power? Why or why not?

Date : _____

How are you feeling today?
Name something you're looking
forward to today.

Date : _____

Describe your past self (who you used to be).

_____

_____

_____

_____

_____

_____

_____

_____

_____

_____

_____

_____

_____

_____

_____

_____

_____

Date : _____

Describe your future self (who you will be someday).

_____

_____

_____

_____

_____

_____

_____

_____

_____

_____

_____

_____

_____

_____

_____

Date : _____

Do you read/watch the news? If
so, how does it impact your
mental health? If not, why not?

Date : _____

What is your relationship with social
media? How does social media
impact your mental health?

_____

_____

_____

_____

_____

_____

_____

_____

_____

_____

_____

_____

_____

_____

_____

_____

Date : _____

How do you define success?

306

Do you consider yourself to be successful? Why or why not?

Date : _____

What was the best gift you received as a child?

Date : _____

What was the best gift you
received as an adult?

Name someone or something you're happy you let go. Explain.

Who is the first person you usually talk to everyday? List 3 positive qualities about that person.

Date : _____

Name something that makes
you laugh so hard you get tears
in your eyes.

312

Name someone whose life you impacted in a positive way. What did you do for them?

Date : _____

What can you do this week to express gratitude to others?

Date : _____

Which of your character traits are you most grateful for?

Name something you enjoy
doing alone. Why do you prefer
to do this alone?

Date : _____

316

Describe something you prefer
to do with others rather than
by yourself.

Date : _____

What freedoms are you
grateful for?

Date : _____

What about your upbringing are you most grateful for?

Date : _____

Who do you love unconditionally?
Who loves you unconditionally?

Name three of your relationship
deal breakers.

_____

_____

_____

_____

_____

_____

_____

_____

_____

_____

_____

_____

_____

_____

_____

Date : _____

Describe a time when you had your heart broken, or you were dumped, stood-up, etc.

322

Describe a time when someone
you thought was a friend
treated you poorly.

Date : _____

Thinking about #322, how did
you handle this situation?

_____

_____

_____

_____

_____

_____

_____

_____

_____

_____

_____

_____

_____

_____

_____

_____

Date : _____

If you knew you couldn't fail,
name something you would do?

Are you more of a leader or a follower? Explain.

326

When people complain about you, what do they say? How do you feel about that?

Finish this sentence: I wish my partner would...

Finish this sentence: I wish my friends would...

Date : _____

Finish this sentence: I wish I never...

Date : _____

Finish this sentence: I wish I
could see...

Date : _____

What expectation do others have of you that you wish they didn't?

What is the one thing you need
to focus on now, that will make
your future better?

Date : _____

Name three things you'd like
to be a part of your daily life.

Name something that you
happily spend money on, but
others might judge you for it.

As a teenager were you a rule-breaker or a rule-follower? Are you the same or different now?

Other than your job, what takes up most of your time? Are you happy about that?

Date : _____

List your 10 favorite things (could be a person, a place, a food, a song, an activity, etc.).

338

What task have you been putting off? How can you get it done within the next week?

Date : _____

Has your life always been on the path leading you to where you are now? Explain.

Is there something you're thinking about doing that you haven't discussed with anyone yet?

Name something you've always
wanted to try or do, that you
never have.

What are your core values?

How have you contributed to
the situation in your life that
makes you most unhappy?

Do you know someone who is in need? What can you do to make things easier for them?

Date : _____

Thinking back on your life, are you more often the victim or the hero?

_____

_____

_____

_____

_____

_____

_____

_____

_____

_____

_____

_____

_____

_____

_____

_____

_____

Name a time when you told a lie.
What would have happened if
you told the truth?

Name something you're angry about, but haven't dealt with.

Would you raise your children the way your parents raised you? Why or why not?

Date : _____

Describe what you're wearing when you feel most attractive.

_____

_____

_____

_____

_____

_____

_____

_____

_____

_____

_____

_____

_____

_____

_____

_____

_____

_____

Date : _____

Write about something you really want, but you fear you'll never have.

351

Write about something you
thought you wanted, but you're
glad didn't work out.

Describe a family story that
gets told repeatedly when your
family gets together.

Write about your first week of college or your first week at your first job.

What advice would you give to future generations?

Date : _____

What makes you feel strong or powerful?

356

What can you do today that you didn't think you could do a year ago?

Date : _____

How have you been feeling this
week? What's been causing
these feelings?

_____

_____

_____

_____

_____

_____

_____

_____

_____

_____

_____

_____

_____

_____

_____

_____

_____

Date : _____

Name something you can do to
stay focused on your
daily/weekly goals.

_____

_____

_____

_____

_____

_____

_____

_____

_____

_____

_____

_____

_____

Date : _____

Name something that tends to
break your focus or make you
feel discouraged.

Date : _____

Who do you go to when you
need to make a big decision?
Why do you trust this person?

Date : _____

Are you truly happy when other
people accomplish the things
you wish to accomplish?

Date : _____

362

What are the three greatest moments of your life?

Date : _____

363

Whatever it is that you're trying to achieve, do you believe you can achieve it?

Why did you start journaling?

Date : _____

What did you learn from your
journaling experience?

_____

_____

_____

_____

_____

_____

_____

_____

_____

_____

_____

_____

_____

_____

_____

_____

_____

_____

Printed in Great Britain
by Amazon

14555977R00210